Twent10ne

ten in twenty-one

e.c.crisostomo

BookLeaf Publishing

India | USA | UK

Dedication

To my family,

Dad, you have shown me true strength;
your selflessness for our family
is something I can't appreciate enough.

Mom, you have raised my brother and I
with so much love and I can't thank you enough
for always reflecting Christ.

Kuya, I will read this to you aloud,
you have always been a beautiful reminder
of God's nearness and miracles everyday.

To my friends and church families,

You are and will always be part of my story.
Thank you for encouraging me.

To my Constant,

You will always be highlighted in every story
and every word I write.
You are my Inspiration.
Always.

Preface

This poetry book is one of my first ever attempts
in publishing and publicizing my works.
I share the precious memories of my first trip to the
Philippines
after being away for about 10 years.
This book contains poems that capture
a longing for a home that once was,
the nervousness that comes with not knowing
if that home still exists,
and rediscovering what makes a home
in one of the most festive
but also coldest seasons of the year.

My hope is that through this creative process
I can somehow allow
those that inspired each work to enjoy my way
of documenting our meaningful meetups
and for readers to find themselves seen
(or relate to similar stories)
in my adventures and self-reflections as well.

Acknowledgements

In relationship we find our rest, this vacation taught me that although relationships take hard work, they are also what makes life more colorful. I thank my dad, mom, Kuya, if it weren't for you three I would've been on my own missing you guys. Thank you for tagging along. I thank Veronica, our driver, and her husband too, for driving us for our arrivals and departure. You are such a blessing to my family! I thank Tito Lito and Tita Lorna for also accommodating me and welcoming me back with open arms and warm food, not to mention caring for our valuables while we were away.

I thank Tita Carol, Tita Malou, Tito Roger, Ate Yhe, Kuya Rome, and baby Iza (who I have yet to meet) -- my family though not in blood. You made me feel so at home again in the Philippines, and you all gave so much of your time and sacrificed your comfort for us to enjoy our stay. I thank Tita Edna, who is also my dentist, for her professional services but also for helping me step out of my comfort zone. I thank Ate Kim for being game to go anywhere and try something new for a change. I thank my church family at JILGM, for the wonderful Christmas service and also the raffles and games; they were indeed exciting and reminiscent of all the fun we've ever had. I also thank Ate Jane, Kuya Bong, and Samuel for being with us during Christmas, and bringing that big pizza to complete the festivities.

I thank Janine for the friendship we shared during high school and how we've come to grow in our understanding of one another. I thank Lystra for your friendship that still keeps in touch no matter the years that have passed, and I'm truly happy for you and how your life is moving forward. I thank Jojie, my anak, for always being that positive energy and that bright smile in the room. I'm so proud you have grown into an even more beautiful and kinder version of yourself. I thank Nicole, my Twinnie, for being the twin sister I know God gifted me to find. We didn't get to go to Japan, but our date in BGC was pretty close. I thank Sofia and Jed for the friendship and open arms; you both blessed me with so much laughter and I loved catching up with the both of you. Extra thanks to Sofia, too, for lending her creative eye to the selection of my book cover. I thank Mia for being such a steadfast presence in my life. I'm so grateful you honor me with a VIP pass for access to both the front and backstage to your life. I thank Tito Tim, Tita Carol, Chelsea, and Emil for your hospitality towards me every time I visit. I hope I get to return that to you all one day. I thank Jhannah and Francis for the fun time we had in the mall of my childhood but also how you shared your stories willingly and how you showed me that you two are gentle souls caring for and loving each other. I was most reassured by that during our meetup.

I thank each of the Crisostomo clans and my Titos, Titas, and cousins, there are so many of you that I wish I could list here by name. I really do sincerely thank you for such a wonderful reunion and how you've welcomed me and my family so warmly. I love spending time with each of you and I'm so glad I feel more connected after working on the digital family tree. Special shoutout to Kuya Jan Thomas "Jabbar" for not only driving us back and forth but also being such a wonderful tour guide and helping hand.

I thank all the new people I met throughout this vacation because you have been so kind and inviting. Your conversations have also stuck with me. And for the friends I didn't get to meet because of limited time, I apologize but also I hope we can plan something at another time. I am grateful for the friendship you continue to bless me with!

I thank my friends, leaders, and sisters-in-Christ who encouraged me to publish my poetry. I wouldn't have taken this brave step if it weren't for your expressed support for me and my writings.

I thank Instagram and online ads and to the publishers here at BookLeaf for their idea of a 21-day writing challenge so I can finally begin this journey of publishing my work. It's a wonderful first step!

Last but not the least, I thank my Jesus, my Constant, for being my Strength and my Joy. I get to live the full life because of You! With You, I am satisfied.

1. same changes

i imagine the day
you welcome me
as i step foot
on the same soil

i am nervous
like someone on a first date
of a lover that once was
and is now back
or a friend i've missed
and haven't seen for so long

questions fill my mind:
what changed...
...and what stayed the same?

i often wonder:
will i recognize you?
will you welcome me
with the same hospitality?
will i be shocked
or pleasantly surprised
or possibly even both
by the changes --

our changes?

i'm excited, now at year 10
to get to know you once again.

2. attachments

i have 2 lists:
things i need to bring
and things to buy as gifts

i also have 10-worth of
videos and photos
to let you know

where i've been
and where i am going

3. christmas in lights

three different plane rides
26 hours, midnight cover
no sign of life beyond
the black rounded window.

sitting and twitching
when finally closing
red and green lights
all glimmering
from below,
the stars inverting.

as soon as we land,
i hear them cheering:
is this what it feels like
to find myself reeling
with excitement and fear
mingling because
i'm both old and new here?

then the first face I see:
one of the people that reared me;
my heart leapt with glee.
fitting all of 10 packages,

we ride in this traffic mess

but all I could notice were lights
aglow
again green, red, and gold
shining
as if to greet me here:

back to the land
where christmas spirit
is seen in every street and building.

4. bowl of ramen

"what a miracle"
i thought as i read
your offer to meet with me
again.

i thought you had forgotten me
now that you're older
but here you were replying
to the text message
i've second-guessed.

i finally see you at the pickup
you drive me through waze
we park and you mention
i haven't really changed.

i also noticed you haven't changed.

we go find a spot to eat
i take your suggestion
because I haven't been
in a long time
in 10 years --
or maybe two.

back then I was so sure
it would be a *we*;
what once was three
became *a one and two.*

we patch things up
our feelings raw;
each with
a bowl of ramen.

5. walking in venice

walking alone in all the new
the replica of a floating city
i flowed about like the waters blue
taking in *all that i* **see**.

i step out of the store
looking about for where you were
i see you rushing right before
i beheld you, *you* **held** *me* there.

linking each other's arms
you perfectly plan our leisurely stroll
pictures and poses, books and stars
here i watch you **all** *enthralled.*

you've gotten so pretty
i told you but you laughed it off
saying you just had money
we **laugh** but i meant it all.

you've grown into the woman
i **knew** *you would be*
i wish i had been by your side
reflecting on all the things i see.

you've both changed
yet stayed the same
though we've aged
we speak our **unchanged** nicknames.

10 years have passed
yet *i* **missed** *you* just as much
i realized it there and then
while i wave goodbye
as you now march ahead.

6. summer anime

my heart skips
though i am steady

i wait before an eye clinic
hoping i spot you quickly
you appear and we embrace
i've been longing to see you
face-to-face

we walk and talk, **side-by-side**
we reach the bookstore
looking to find books from my list
but here we were
writing stories of our own

we **look and look and look**
trying to find hidden treasure
in the shelves we've skimmed over
we come out famished

we **walk and walk and walk**
trying to side where to eat
we settle for a bento store
it was like no time had passed us at all

i treat you there but you insist
to treat me to dessert at least

you and i, **arm-in-arm**
because your eyes can't look too far
we stand in line for frozen green yogurt
and while we wait, boom it goes
colors painted the night sky
they were so close and jokes began
we talked about comets and fireworks
how we met, our own japan

we sat and talked till time exhausts
you need to pack: a trip up north
I walked you back
it's time to part at 10
i hug you tight
then waved and smiled

but in my heart
i don't let go
on you, **i keep my sight**

7. nameless alchemist

chasing after 10s
talking 'bout legends not ours
no name, we part ways

8. church fam

i still know where things go
the same a/c since years ago
people warmly greeting me
having gone around
while a *song plays* aloud
caught me off guard
there were some things
i had forgotten
we all eat some *pancit*
and scattered round we sit
the party starts, *raffles won*
my brother's name announced
i usually never win these games
 the 10th it was, they call my name
i get some cash which is quite great
we play some games, we trio lose,
heavy-handed, i guess none could choose
practice *stacking*
we also don't win at reciting
siopao, siomai, suman
we take a group picture
with virtual brothers and sisters
then we talk, all caught up
till it was late afternoon

the warmth i felt that day
reminded me of growing up
with a tight-knit church
where everyone belonged

9. duo reunites

the duo returns

she waits for her to come in view
a gloomy sky, not a hint of blue
she walks and calls in a few
the duo meet as they cross the queue

the duo catches up

both tell each other 10 adventures
lessons they learned and other treasures
and some friends lost in life's bleachers
but both grateful, relationship nurtures

the duo parts ways

again they say goodbye not forever
talk of meeting someday, near future
one recalls the past with an aperture
the other looks for another clincher

10. birthday

this was what I missed:
the round glass wooden table
where 10 food items are plated
and even more people are seated

we all spend the christmas evening
talking, eating, watching, resting
we couldn't even wait for midnight
stomachs were full
but even more so, our hearts

though some of us are missing tonight
it's good to be back under one roof
where i had the best christmases
when i got to spend them
with all of you

i thank Jesus
on His birthday
for bringing us all
together
this year
and forever

11. little sunshine

her smile
was the sun
radiated
warming my skin
her arms
were the party
waving and celebrating
even from afar
illuminating my heart
no days
seemed
to pass
between us
me and you
walking
eating
talking
around were
others
though
here i was
orbiting
around you

we end
at 10
yet
i dream
with you
again

12. kkb

we have breakfast with your family
we get ready to meet our friends
we ride the taxi and talk about churches
we stop at a friend's house to drop a luggage
we walk and talk 5 mins to the mall
we decide what place to eat at, that's all
we arrive at the k-bbq place, 5 mins
we wait for the meat and our friend
we see her come, our table full again
we laugh and cry and reminisce
we cook and kkb, while giving gifts
we walk out the heavy meal and eat again
we laugh some more, hug, snap a photo and
we realize someone paid the tab
we look around for pokemon stickers
we find a snowy christmas angle
we bobbed and sang along to miniso
we got in line for some jolli soft serve
we go back to get the luggage
we hug again and take the grab
we stop at the condo and hug at last
we will miss each other once again
we will try to meet years less than 10

13. baby pink

i wish i was there
when you gave your "yes"
i wish i was there
in person, with everyone else
when you said your "i do"
i wish i was with you
in those milestones
we used to dream about
things you were uncertain then
but God showed up
now it's here
after all these wishes
i can finally be
here with you now
as you carry your baby
i'm glad i didn't have to miss
celebrating you in baby pink
but then again i wish i'd left at 10
but i'm back here too early then
i wish i was there
to see your baby
but know i'll be back
showering her with gifts aplenty

14. mini japan

the practice starts at early 8
i wake up and plan to take a shower
i realized i had to heat up some water
you three wake up a little later
i'm just excited i get to tag along in the matter

we all read and discuss God's Word, end in prayer
each of you begin to take your positions
as I sit in the corner, i read and sometimes chatter
once we're done packing up, we three began our walk
we buy some potato corner fries from the street across

we ride a grab to get to gala food park,
a mini japan in the philippines,
here are 10 depictions:
the line for yukata rentals
the bamboo displays
the shiny stone floors
the overpowering smell of varnish
the stalls with flags written in hiragana with translations
the anime character statues lined up on walls
the aesthetic and kawaii decorations
the plastic sakura trees and orange maples
the hot spring themed bathrooms

some of the stalls sold filipino comfort food
a mixture of home and overseas culture
we talked about how we should come back
at night, months later when they open the rooftop
however we found no desserts around
so we crossed the street and found
another mall and went to cb & tl
sitting and chatting till it was dark
we talked about dreams, family, love & life

i missed these all-day hangouts like we've got no plans
but tomorrow i'm leaving, early to travel out of the city

15. ride

early morning
we planned to leave
all packed up and ready,
no skipping beats, we wait for my cousin
who i haven't seen in years, *look at God*
making sure we get to the province with a mission
to bring Jesus and this cousin, we ride down south
and there they were, *the mountains* with forests all
luscious
and full but now there were lots of cafes and restos
blocking the view
even then i still enjoyed *going up and down* and back
again the sights made
my heart skip thinking of an adventure about to begin
we made a stop when
my cousin noticed me *taking photos* of the new tall
windmills above the face of the mountains

after that was all a blur, we went zigzag and drowsiness
occurred, we finally arrived but
the sun was nowhere to be found, we arrived at our
generous relative's house a bit wet, no doubt
but we make our way yet again to where we'll have our
small reunion just between my father's siblings and

families,
at the *house i visited,* every christmas when my mother,
brother, and i got to travel, i finally meet my niece and
nephew and the fur babies of their aunt and uncle, my
nephew proved to be *skilled in fishing* with a simple pole
and some bread abaiting, i help prepare the charcuterie
my mom envisioned, ate > 10 pieces with my cousins, i
hear the *singing voice* of my niece and her mother while
feeding my brother, my cousins and i end up helping my
mother put chocolates in respective bags, we end the
night by *taking pictures* of each family until we
completed the line up

i have to admit it was very lovely to spend time with the
relatives *i grew up with,* we end up going back
to our designated stay as soon as the *tiny crabs* came
above the land approaching, we arrived
knocked out, comfy with the a/c, **expectant** for
tomorrow's larger reunion *awaiting*

16. red and green

red and green plaid
christmas colors
blood and life
yes and no
opposites that go together
this time we wear them
as a symbol of
our families reuniting

this one day
which we planned months ago
two families are hosting
both pray in unity
for this event to mean more
we start with songs of worship
then my dad rapping
talking about how Jesus
makes life better
if we accept Him
next came my aunt sharing
then they honored our pillars
the elders of a previous generation

we now eat and get ready
to play what seems like 10 games
each 10-11 families represented
blessing the children, students, servers
my nephew all smiles from
the cash he had earned and won
we end with a few dance videos
now the time has come
we take our final group photos
and say our farewells and see you agains

we ride back to our designated spaces
the family tree full of names i've listed
now come with all these stories and faces

17. in between

the rain hasn't stopped
but today it did
what a miracle it brought
now we can go swim

we walk down the shore
warm ash brown sand
i try to avoid stepping on
10 prickly rocks and seaweed

i missed the pacific
the calm and steady waves
i bring my brother's feet
up to the crashing water

it pulls us in softly
but releases us swiftly

then i wonder how such
a mighty force full of power
can be so tame in a matter
of seconds and minutes
yet unpredictable as the storms
come weathering down

reminding us again humans
that God is ruler over the oceans
though we question life's troubles
when friends leave us in untimely hours
God is still good and sovereign in power
teaching us that life is the ebb and the flow
just as He was brought high and really low
grateful He didn't stay below
so we may be wherever He goes

18. childhood to new

childhood best friends
we set aside time to meet
for the last see-you-again
this time with your s.o.
the one you like to talk about
the new best friend

childhood mega mall
once familiar now a stranger
the floors and frames all the same
though >10 features have been changed
we go up and down the escalators
the new purlieu

some things have changed, yes
but important things remain
though you're in a new season
please know, i'm always at your disposal
we grew up together and even now
we grow even when we're apart

i'm happy you met a special one
to share the wins and loss of life
just know i'll always be the one

here with you no matter what
from childhood to the new
i am here for you

19. repeat

balikbayan training:
always buy and stock during sales
like valentines and halloween for chocolates and candies
black fridays, memorial day, and cyber monday
for others:
shoes, electronics, toys, books, bath&body,
canned goods, etc.
make a list of the people you want to meet
think about the gifts you wanna give
but also prepare some extras just in case
collect paper gift bags and crepe paper (if feeling fancy)
gather some cards or notes to attach to the gifts
put them all in a balikbayan box, ship months
before arrival
so the box will be delivered when you're there
once in the philippines, open the box, arrange the items
empty your luggage, leave your 10 items behind
give to loved ones and friends and admire their smiles
now it's time to buy philippine goods and delicacies
for the people back in the usa, go to the mall and check
buy a few cheap items for yourself
make the list of the people you will be meeting
but also prepare some extras just in case
make sure they all fit your now empty luggage

and give again with leftover
paper gift bags and crepe paper
admire their smiles, take in their appreciation
take the process all in, and once again
go on repeat

20. two-day layover

all alone
i try my best
hold back my tears
i wait in line
i check my bags
line up again
the tsa i make my way
i wait for hours
i eat alone
and read my book
my flight postponed
i wait some more
till gate e is called
my carry on, i put up
in an empty compartment
i sit and an attendant smiles
my seatmate's elbow out of line
i eat three meals and here i was
dubai at last, a little lost
i stay wandering, finding a pod
a fellow filipino told me a spot
i grab some food and buy kunafa
check in and sleep thru the night
i wake up, and take a paid shower

i wait and wait at 10 for my hour
i eat mcdonalds, watching anime
i sip my tea and finish my book
i board again, and watch and watch
thought i'd see an airport romance
but clearly not, i watch my series
it was nice, they offered pictures
complimentary in flight
i said why not, the attendant teased
the plane now stopped at athens, greece
again we lined up for tsa
it's nice to know airports here fill up
water bottles with no extra fee
i made a friend but never got
her contact info, but it was nice
to wait with someone for a while
we board again this time toward
though sad i was, bittersweet to say
farewell to the home that once was
but also to say
hi to the home i've made again

21. all the places

looking back i used to be
frightened of the idea
of traveling solo without my family
but now i've flown back and forth by myself
this third time and i've never felt
more confident now and even somehow
i don't seem to fear staying home all by myself,
though i have to admit
there were times when being home alone
meant crying because i miss my true home,
the company i kept every time i needed rest,
my family and friends
when i was in the philippines they surrounded me
though i liked my privacy,
i realized i liked the noise
even more, the places were always full
with things to do now i'm stuck doing work
and when i return, even more work
i can't believe i also went
straight to work with a 5-hour rest
good thing the jet lag didn't hit too much,
but later on it'll catch up
though i really couldn't stop thanking God
because i made it when i couldn't visit

during the pandemic, then went for further studies
i am glad that 10 years passed without a hitch,
thought it was a blink
but then again
now i see i've become more of an adult than i'd ever been

the little girl all scared for the future
when she boarded that aircraft
was now the woman living the future
she'd always dreamed of

albeit, some sidetracks and detours along the way but
she made it to the end anyway,
but this is only the beginning
her journeying keeps going,
and she can't wait to see all she's becoming
and all the places she's **belonging,**
wherever she stays and dreams.